SAINT
BRENDAN

EDITED AND PRESENTED
BY IAIN MACDONALD

FLORIS BOOKS

First published in 1992 by Floris Books

British Library CIP Data available

ISBN 0-86315-141-8

Printed in Great Britain
by Courier International, East Kilbride

Contents

Introduction

St Brendan's long life-span lasted from about 486 to 578. This period saw great changes taking place throughout Europe.

At that time Ireland was peopled by the Gaels (Scoti). They were divided into clans but each clan owed allegiance to the High King of Ireland at Tara. St Patrick (389-461) had already brought Christianity to Ireland, and by St Brendan's time this religion was well established throughout Ireland.

To the Britons who peopled what is now Wales and England, the Romans had already introduced Christianity, but since 411 the Romans had withdrawn their legions and the Britons were now exposed to the invasions of the pagan Angles, Jutes and Saxons.

Gaul too was thoroughly Christian, but there also the Romans were in trouble and the indigenous Gauls were facing the onslaught of the Germanic peoples from the East. The most successful and significant of these invasions was that of the Franks under their king, Clovis, who in St Brendan's lifetime established his kingdom in Northern France with his capital in Paris. Clovis himself became a zealous

Christian and did much to further the Christian religion in France.

Such briefly is the historical background to the life and activity of St Brendan. Brendan was born at Annagh on Tralee Bay about 486. He became a monk and later an abbot (Abbot of Ardfert) and he founded the monastery of Clonfert in County Galway in 561. His travels took him to many parts of Ireland, to Iona (to visit St Columba), to Wales and Britain, and to Gaul. He died around the year 580.

The Voyage (Navigatio) of St Brendan, whatever its historical basis, caught the imagination of the medieval world. The story was well-known. Indeed over a hundred Latin manuscripts of the Navigatio have survived to our day as well as others translated or written in other languages. Before Columbus' discovery of America, medieval maps showed Brendan's Island of Promise out in the Atlantic Ocean.

Hardly less has the Voyage of St Brendan claimed the interest of modern scholars. Great endeavours have been made to establish the identity of the islands mentioned in the Navigatio; and some even go so far as to suggest that Brendan actually sailed to America long before Columbus or the Norsemen; this view was enthusiastically upheld by Tim Severin who con-

structed a leather boat on traditional principles and sailed across the Atlantic in 1977.

But is it not possible that Brendan's search for "The Promised Land of the Saints" was a voyage of the soul, in the same way as the Quest of the Holy Grail can be seen as an adventure of inner development? There do appear to be many similar elements: boats which move of their own accord, bringing the traveller to an pre-ordained destination; holy monks or hermits who act as guides; the significance of the great religious festivals such as Easter and Pentecost, and frequent reference to the daily rhythm of the canonical hours (Prime, Terce, Sext, and so on).

Many scholars have worked on the various Latin and Irish manuscripts of the Navigatio. In 1910 Charles Plummer published his book Vitae Sanctorum Hiberniae which contains the "Vita prima sancti Brendani," based on the Latin manuscripts which were available to him. He estimated that those manuscripts were no older than the thirteenth century. He did not translate his publication into English. The now standard edition of the Latin manuscripts was published in 1959 by Carl Selmar, and translated into English by J.F.Webb in Penguin Books (1965) and by John O'Meara (1976) who suggests that the Latin version was written as early as 800 AD.

In 1922 Plummer published Bethada Náem n'Erenn *(Lives of Irish Saints) in which he edited and translated the Irish-Gaelic text of the "Life of St Brendan." This text was based mainly on an Irish-Gaelic manuscript written by Michael O'Clery dated 1629. It is from this English translation of the Irish text that the present extracts are made. However, we should mention that in Plummer's collection there is a further, much shorter, account of the Voyage, called "The Twelve Apostles of Ireland," which has some interesting variations from O'Clery's version and some wonderfully descriptive writing.*

The life of St Brendan

Many were the wonderful things which happened at the birth of St Brendan, son of Findlug of Alltraighe Caille. Before his birth his mother dreamed that her bosom was full of pure gold. On the night of his birth the local bishop, Bishop Erc, saw Alltraighe Caille "all in one great blaze..., and an attendance of angels in shining white garments all round that land."

Realizing that this was a child marked out for a special destiny, when Brendan was a year old, Bishop Erc gave him to a nun called Ita to foster. Ita cared for him for five years. Thereafter he was under the tutelage of Bishop Erc with whom he learned the canon of the Old and New Testaments, but it was an angel who taught him the rule of the saints of Ireland. Then Brendan was moved by the words of the gospel where it says: "Everyone who has left houses or brothers or sisters or father or mother or children or lands, for my name's sake, will receive a hundredfold, and inherit eternal life."

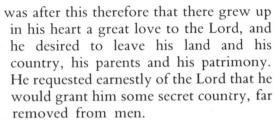t was after this therefore that there grew up in his heart a great love to the Lord, and he desired to leave his land and his country, his parents and his patrimony. He requested earnestly of the Lord that he would grant him some secret country, far removed from men.

It happened then that Brendan was in the place called Leim na Subaltaige, when there came to him a certain holy man named Barinthus, son's son to King Niall. And as Brendan was making many inquiries of him, he prostrated himself on the ground mourning and weeping. Brendan raised him from the ground, and kissing him said to him: "It were fitter for thee to rejoice than to mourn; and by God's Passion I adjure thee to tell us some of the words of God, and satisfy our souls."

And after such converse between them the man began to tell him of a certain island, and said as follows: "I had a son named Mernoc, and he fled from me, because he did not wish to remain in the same place with me. And he found an island near a certain mountain called Sliabh na Cloiche. And some time afterwards, when it had been shown to me that he had many monks with him, and that many miracles were manifested through him, I went on a visit to him; and when I came within three days' journey of him, he came to meet me with the brethren, for God had revealed to him my coming.

"And when we reached the island, the brethren came to us out of their cells, like a swarm of bees; and though their dwellings were divided from one another, there was no division in their converse, or counsel, or affection. And their only victuals were apples and nuts, and roots of such kinds of herbs as they found. And the brethren used to go to their separate cells from Compline till cockcrow.

"And I and my son traversed the island, and after we had gone over it, he took me with him to the shore where was a boat; and he said to me: 'Dear father, get into the boat,' said he, 'that we may go and see the island which is called *The Land of the Saints*, which God is to promise to men who shall come after us.' And when we had entered the boat, a mist fell upon us, so that we could hardly see the prow of our boat.

"And when we had spent the space of an hour of the day in this way, a great light came upon us, and we saw the island in resplendent beauty, full of fragrant apples and blossom; and there was no single herb or tree among them which

was not laden with fruit. And then we brought
the boat to land in the island. And we were
traversing it for the space of fifteen days, and
could not find any end to it. And the stones of
the island were all jewels. And at the end of the
fifteenth day we found a stream which traversed
the island, and we did not know what to do as to
crossing the stream. And we awaited the counsel
of God.

"And as we were setting forth, we saw
coming to us a man of radiant beauty, who
greeted us by our own proper names, and said:
'Beloved brothers, God has revealed this land to
you, and this is the half of the island, and it is not
permitted to you to go beyond it; so return to
the place whence ye came.' And when he had
said this, we asked him whence he came, and
what his own name was.

"The man said: 'What makes you ask me this?
to it were fitter for you to inquire about this
island and its history than about mine; for ye see
it now without lack of fruit or flower, and thus
it is since the beginning of the world. And ye
need no food or drink; for ye have been a year in
this land, and have not tasted food or drink all
that time, and further ye have not needed rest or
sleep, nor has night or other darkness befallen

you during that time. So then day unending and unceasing will last here without darkness for ever, for our Lord Jesus Christ is the light and splendour of it. And if men did not transgress the commandments of their Lord, they would remain in this delight everlastingly.'

"And when we heard this, we experienced great sorrow, and intense regret; and when we had finished our mourning we began to return to our boat. And the holy man accompanied us to the brink of the shore; and when we had entered our boat, he was taken from our sight, so that we knew not whither he had betaken himself from us.

"And after we had set out thus, we passed through the same mist which we spoke of above. And we made no stop or stay till we came to the brink of the island from which we set out previously. And when the brethren saw us, they were filled with immeasurable joy and gladness at our coming to them, and began to question us as to what had befallen us during the time of our absence; and they said: 'O holy fathers, why have ye left your sheep to wander in this island without a shepherd? And our abbot has often gone away from us for a month or a fortnight, or a week or less.'

"And my son, Mernoc, tried to comfort the brethren. And I said to them afterwards," said Barinthus, " 'Think not anything but what is unquestionably good, for your converse is good, and your dwelling is hard by Paradise, and near to you is the island which is called *the Promised Land of the Saints.* There is never any night, and the day never ends. And Mernoc, your abbot, has often been there, and the angels of God protect that island. And have ye not perceived by the scent of our garments that we have been in Paradise?'

"The brethren said: 'Ah, dear father,' said they, 'we perceived that ye had been in Paradise, by the goodly smell of your garments; for often has our abbot himself been there, and the smell of his raiment has been meat to us for the space of forty days.' And, O Brendan," said Barinthus, "I remained a fortnight in that place with my son, without eating or drinking, and at the end of forty days I returned to my brethren and my own cell."

When Brendan and the brethren heard this, they bowed their heads to the ground, and praised God greatly, and said: *"Benedictus Deus,"* that is, Blessed is God in His own gifts, and holy in all His works, in that he has revealed so many

miracles as these to His servants, and has fed us
to the full this day with spiritual food.

And after this mutual converse Brendan bade
his family go with him to spiritual refreshment
and renewal. When the night was passed, and
Brendan had given his blessing to Barinthus, the
latter returned to his own place of abode.

And when he had departed, Brendan collected
fourteen brethren of his congregation, and went
with them to a secluded place; and among them
was an elect youth, illustrious in good works,
engaged in the praise of God from the beginning
of his life to the end. And whoever wishes to
acquire a knowledge of his acts, let him read his
youthful deeds; and the person to whom we
allude is Machutus. Brendan spoke to the
brethren, and said: "O beloved fellow citizens,"
said he, "I am asking of you counsel and help,
for my heart and thoughts are all fixed on one
single desire, if it be God's desire, to seek the
land which Barinthus told us of, the land which
God has promised to the men who shall come
after us. And what counsel do ye give me
hereon?"

When Brendan had made known his desire to
the brethren, they all said with one voice:
"Beloved father," said they, "the counsel that

thou willest, is the counsel that we will. And
have we not left our own fathers for thee? and
have we not left our own inheritance for thyself?
and did we not surrender our bodies into thy
hands? And therefore we are ready to take death
or life together with thee. There is but one thing
besides. Let us seek to ascertain the will of the
holy Father, and to fulfil it."

So Brendan with his family determined to
hold a fast of forty days and nights to the Lord,
that he would prosper them, and guide them to
the end in every path in which they were to go.

Brendan slept after this, and heard the voice of
an angel from heaven saying: "Arise, Brendan,"
said he, "that which thou hast requested thou
shalt receive of God, that is to visit *the Land of
Promise* at last."

Thereupon Brendan arose, and his heart
rejoiced at the answer of the angel. And he went
to a place apart by himself, and scanned the
ocean on every side of him. And he saw on the
ocean an island wondrous fair with attendance
of angels about it. After this Brendan remained
in that place some time, and slept again a little in
it. The angel of God came to converse with him
once more, and said to him: "Henceforth," said
he, "I will be ever with thee, and I will show

thee one day the fair island which thou hast seen, and which thou desirest to find."

Brendan wept greatly for joy at the answer of the angel, and gave thanks to God.

Brendan then set forth with his company, leaving their blessing with the prior of the monastery which we spoke of previously, who was afterwards Brendan's successor among the brethren. And Brendan then went westwards, and fourteen brethren with him, till he reached the island of a holy father named Enda of Aran; and made a stay of three days and three nights in the island.

Then Brendan with his company went into the most distant part of his paternal territory; but he would not approach his father or mother, or go near them, but went to the summit of a lofty mountain near the ocean where their boat was. And that place was thenceforth called Suide Brenainn (Brendan's Seat). They said that it was time for them to find that island, and they went to their boat to strengthen it with iron and ox hides; and they then placed in Brendan's boat equipment of every kind sufficient for two other boats. And they smeared their joinings within and without with myrrh and bitumen, and pitch and rosin.

And when the boat was ready, Brendan bade his company embark in the name of the Father, Son, and Holy Ghost. He himself remained behind them alone on the shore, and blessed the harbour on either side. And after this he saw three monks of his family coming towards him, and they fell on their knees before him, and said: "O holy father," said they, "for the love of God let us go with thee where thou goest, or else we will starve ourselves, for we have vowed to make our pilgrimage with thee as long as we live."

When the father, Brendan, saw their distress, he said to them: "Get into the boat, for I know in what sort ye have come. Good are the works of one man of you, and God has prepared a good place for him; but he has prepared additional punishment for the rest of you."

So after this converse Brendan entered his boat, and his company entered their two other boats. And on this wise were Brendan's boats, with three rows of oars to each boat, and sails of the skins of animals both wild and domesticated, and twenty men in each boat.

Then came a jester to Brendan, and knelt before him, and said to him: "O Brendan," said he, "take me with thee for God's sake, and pity my wretchedness, that I may go with thee."

Brendan took him with him for God's sake, and embarked in his boats with sixty men as writings say:

Sixty men of them in the fleet;
They laboured not on Sunday;
Their minds were fixed on the dear Creator,
Praising the King of the heavenly palace.

After this they went on the surface of the sea and mighty ocean and hoisted their sails above their boats, and the wind carried them to the port of Aran again. And Pupa, and Enda of Aran, and Ronad came to see the fleet.

The first voyage

The island of mice

Brendan bade farewell to the saints of Aran, and left a blessing with them, and they sailed on due west across the ocean, and saw after a while at a distance from them a notable fair island. And they steered their boats towards it, till they reached the brink of it. And they saw the shore full of hideous furry mice as large as cats. The brethren asked Brendan: "What do yonder mice

want?" said they. "Their desire is to eat and
devour us," said Brendan.

Thereupon was revealed to Brendan that it
was the death hour of the jester who was in the
boat with them. So he said to him: "Arise," said
he, "and take the body and blood of Christ, and
depart to the eternal life, for I hear the song of
the angels calling thee to them."

Then the mind of the jester rejoiced at this
saying: "Ah, Lord," said he, "what good have I
done that I should be taken to heaven so
speedily?"

Brendan answered and said that it was fitting
that he should fulfil the will of God.

So when he had received the body and blood
of Christ, his spirit leapt forth and was straight-
way borne up with great joy to heaven, where is
Jesus Christ with the nine orders of heaven
about him.

*The company did not land upon this island, but the
body of the jester who had come aboard at the last
moment was put ashore and the huge mice devoured it.
Afterwards Brendan buried the bones and they sailed
on. For forty days they continued to sail until they
came to another island, lofty, stony and sandy. There
they landed. They were met by a little dog who took*

them to a house where they found food. One of
Brendan's monks was tempted by the devil to steal a
golden bridle. On discovering this, Brendan expelled
the devil, and soon afterwards the monk died. They
then returned to their boat and sailed on.

They eventually came to an island known as the
Paradise of Birds where they met a holy man, who
afterwards is called the Procurator. In a monastic
community we can understand the procurator to be the
general administrator or factor, but there is another
meaning whereby this Latin word is used for the
Greek word "parakletos," the Paraclete, the advo-
cate, comforter and guide. Thus Brendan's meeting
with the Procurator gains a deeper significance.

ne day as they were traversing the ocean,
they saw an island at some distance from them. And they
steered their boat towards it, and
landed on it. And on making a
circuit of the island, they found
goodly streams full of fish in it. Brendan said to
the brethren: "Let us perform divine service
here, and consecrate the immaculate Lamb to
God, for today is the Supper of our Lord Jesus
Christ."

And they remained thus till Easter Eve; and

they found numerous herds of sheep, large and
pure white, so that they could hardly see the
ground through them for the multitude of the
sheep. Brendan said to them: "Take with you,
brethren, from yonder herds as much as ye
require for Easter."

The brethren then took one of the sheep; and
as they were binding it, the other sheep followed
them thenceforth.

So they prepared all things that they needed
against the venerable day of Easter. Then they
saw one coming towards them, bearing a vessel
full of bread, and with it all that they needed for
their consumption. He set it down before
Brendan, and then threw himself on the ground,
and wept bitterly and said: "O father, though I
am not worthy to feed thee with the work of my
hands, accept this food of me in these holy
days."

And Brendan raised him from the ground,
and kissed him, and asked him: "Where has our
Lord Jesus Christ ordained for us to celebrate
Easter?"

The holy man answered him and said; "Here
are ye to keep this Saturday and vigil, and on
yonder island that ye now see in the offing shall
ye celebrate the Easter Masses."

And having said thus he began to render the service (of the day, that is, the foot washing) to Brendan and the other brethren. And after this they filled their boats with such things as they required. The man then said to Brendan: "Ye cannot carry anything more in your boats; but after eight days I will send you all that ye will need of food and drink till Pentecost."

Brendan said to him: "Knowest thou where we shall be after eight days?"

The holy man said: "Ye will be on that island that ye see yonder tonight, and tomorrow till midday; and then ye shall go to the island which is called *the Paradise of Birds*, and remain there till the octave of Pentecost."

Brendan said: "What makes yonder sheep so large, living as they do in this island?" For each sheep of them was bigger than a fatted ox.

The holy man said: "The reason is that no milk is ever collected from them, nor are their fleeces ever sheared, and no winter or darkness ever comes upon them. And therefore it is that they are of that excessive size, owing to their being always out at grass. Therefore they are larger here than in any other land in the world."

Brendan then put out from land, and rowed with his company till they reached the Paradise

of Birds. And when they reached this island they
landed there. And the island was extraordinary
in appearance, for there were many excellent
fruits there, and marvellous birds discoursing
joyously from the tops of their trees, and little
bees gathering and collecting their harvest and
household store for their own dwellings, and
strangely beautiful streams flowing there, full of
wondrous jewels of every hue. And there were
many churches there, and a monastery in the
middle of the island full of an excellent variety of
things of every hue; and a venerable wise
decorous and devout order in it.

And thus was this monastery, with its own
light burning in it, to wit four lights before the
high altar, and three before the middle altar.
And their chalices were made of crystal. And
there were fourteen seats opposite one another
in the choir, and the abbot's place in the middle
between them; and when the abbot began to
recite a verse the choir responded humbly, and
none of them dared to recite a single verse
except the abbot himself; and none spoke
without permission, except when they were
praising the Lord, unless the abbot permitted;
and even then they did not speak in words, but
by making it known by some intelligible sign

with eye, or lip, or hand, to indicate what they desired to say. And the abbot would write on a tablet with a style every answer that he gave them.

And the abbot said to Brendan after this: "It were time for us to seek our dormitory."

Thereupon they went to Compline; and after reciting Compline the brethren went to their separate cells, and took Brendan's company with them, each brother taking one of them.

And Brendan and the abbot remained in the minster; and while they were there Brendan asked the abbot how men still in human flesh could maintain such silence and quiet. The abbot answered him with humility, and said: "I confess before Christ that it is four score years since we came to this place, and none of us has spoken to another with human voice, save when we are praising the Lord; but it is only through sign of finger or eyes that speech is manifested between us. And further there has been no sickness of body or soul or spirit on any of us all that time."

On hearing this Brendan spoke with tears, and said: "May we remain here for the space of a year?"

The abbot said: "Ye may indeed. Dost thou

not know what was ordained for thee to do
before thou camest hither? For thou must needs
return to thine own place with thy fourteen
brethren; and as to the two others that joined
thee later, one of them will go to his pilgrimage
to the island called *the island of Antonius*, and the
other will go to an evil death, for he will be
damned to hell."

And all this was fulfilled.

*Brendan set off once more on his voyage and was at
sea until Lent. Once again they came upon an island,
the water of which despite Brendan's warning caused
his companions to fall into a deep sleep lasting three
days for some of them. Nevertheless they were able to
replenish their stores and continue their voyage and in
due course discovered that they had returned on their
track to the island of the Procurator.*

The finding of the Paradise of birds

Then they saw an island in the distance, and
Brendan asked his company: "Do ye recognize
yonder island that we see now?" said he.

"We do not indeed," said they.

"It is otherwise with me," said Brendan.
"Yonder is the island on which we were last year

on the day of the Lord's Supper, and on it is the
procurator with whom we were."

When the brethren heard this, they began to
row furiously.

And Brendan said to them: "Do not vex and
rack your limbs. Is not God our Pilot and our
Shipman? Let Him bring us to whatever place
He will."

And they did as Brendan bade; for they let the
boat drift, and God steered them to the island of
the procurator. And when they had landed, the
procurator came to them with great joy; and
kissed the feet of Brendan and of the brethren,
and began loudly to praise the Lord. And when
he had finished his praise, he speedily prepared a
bath for them, for it was the day of the Lord's
Supper at that time. And he clad them all with
new garments, and they celebrated the Lord's
Passion there till Easter Eve.

And when they had recited the service for
Saturday, the procurator said to Brendan:
"Embark, and keep Easter as thou didst last
year. And from Easter onwards go ye to the
Paradise of Birds, and take with you what ye
need of food and drink. And I will pay you a
visit on the second Sunday that is coming."

The brethren departed at this saying to the

island where they had made their Easter the
previous year.

And they departed thence to the Paradise of
Birds, and stayed there till the octave of Pentecost. And the procurator came to them as he had
promised, and brought with him all things
which they required; and they greeted one
another right joyfully, as they were wont.

And when they sat down to table, a bird
alighted that moment on the prow of the ship,
and made music sweet as an organ with its
wings, beating them on the sides of the boat.
And Brendan perceived that it was telling
something; and the bird said: "Four seasons have
been ordained for you during the time of your
journey, to wit, the day of the Lord's Supper
with the procurator, Easter on the back of the
monster, and from Easter to Pentecost with us,
and Christmas in the isle of Ailbe up to Mary's
feast of Candlemas. And at the end of the
seventh year ye shall be borne to the land which
ye are seeking, and ye shall be there forty days,
and after that ye shall be borne to your own
land."

On hearing this Brendan bowed himself to
the ground, and wept and cried and gave praise
and thanks to God, the Creator of all things.

Then when they had finished all these things, the bird returned to its own place.

The procurator said: "I will leave you now, and will come to you again together with all things, that ye will require, as the Holy Procurator came to the apostles of old."

The procurator then departed leaving his blessing with Brendan and the rest; and Brendan remained there during the time appointed him. And when this time expired, Brendan prepared to set forth, and was putting out from the land, when he saw the procurator coming to him with a boat full of provisions, and he gave these to Brendan, and then returned himself the way by which he came. And Brendan was thus on the ocean for the space of forty days and forty nights.

Celebration of Easter on the back of the monster
When, however, Easter drew near, Brendan's company began say to him that he should land for the celebration of Easter. "God is able," said Brendan, "to find a land for us in any place He pleases."

When then Easter came, a great whale raised its shoulders high above the surface of the waves, so that it formed dry land. And then they landed, and celebrated Easter on it. And they were there one day and two nights. When they had entered their boats, the whale dived into the sea at once. However, it was thus that they celebrated Easter to the end of seven years on the back of the sea monster. For when it was near Easter each year, it would lift its back above the sea, forming regular dry land.

Whirlpools threaten Brendan's expedition

Now on one occasion when they were on the wondrous azure-rimmed ocean, they saw deep floodlike currents and black vast whirlpools. Then it seemed as if the boats must be swamped by the greatness of the storm. Each of them began to look in Brendan's face, for the danger in which they were was wondrous great. Brendan lifted up his voice on high, and said: "It is enough, O thou great sea, that I be drowned, but spare this company."

Then the sea became calm at once, and the boiling of the whirlpools abated, and from that time forth it has never injured any one.

Brendan returns to Ireland from his first voyage

Now when Brendan had been five years on this voyage, he returned to his own land and country, as was enjoined him in the island we spoke of. Then the people of his land and tribe came to meet him, and were asking him what profit he had had of his boats; and they gave gifts and treasures to him as to God. And many of them forsaking the world followed Christ. And he did many mighty works and miracles there, and sick folk and prisoners were made whole, and demons and vices were expelled. He then addressed himself to his foster-father, Bishop Erc.

He next went to the place where his foster-mother, Ita, was, and asked her what he should do with reference to his voyage. Ita gave him welcome as she would have bidden welcome to Christ and His apostles, and said to him: "Ah, dearly beloved son, why didst thou go on thy journey without taking counsel with me? For the country which thou art seeking from God, ye will never find on these dead soft skins, for it is a holy consecrated land, and no blood of man was ever shed in it. But let timber boats be made by thee. Belike thou wilt find that land on this wise."

Thereupon Brendan went into the region of Connaught, and an excellent large boat was made by him, and he embarked with his company and people; and they took various herbs and seeds to store the boat withal, and wrights and smiths who had prayed Brendan to let them go with him.

The second voyage

hen Brendan and his company went back again over the surface of the sea and great ocean. They had not been long on this voyage when a sudden sickness seized their smith, and he was at the point of death. Brendan said to him: "Why dost thou wonder?" said he. "Depart to the heavenly kingdom as thou hast ever sought for thyself up to this time; or if thou desirest to remain longer in the world, I will pray to God for thee, and He will be thy health."

The smith said: "I hear the voice of the Lord calling me."

When he had received the body of Christ, and His flesh and blood, he went to heaven. There was then a great questioning among the brethren where they could effect the burial of the corpse, for there was no strand or land near them. Then Brendan bade them bury him in the waves of the sea: "For He who made heaven and earth and the other elements has power over the waves of the sea to fix the corpse immovably in them."

So then the smith was buried among the waves of the sea without drifting to land, and without rising to the surface of the brine, without moving in any direction, as if he were in the ground; as was said:

They bury him, though it was wondrous,
The smith in the ocean,
Amid the waves of the wild sea,
Without sinking under the roar of the billows.

The island of dwarfs

After leaving this place they saw a little insignificant country near them. And as they were landing there, the harbour was filled with demons in the shapes of dwarfs and leprechauns opposing them, whose faces were black as coal. Then said Brendan: "Let go the anchor, for no one can enter this land but one who shall wage human war against demons, and shed blood over them."

They remained there till the end of seven days and seven nights, and they could not draw up their anchor, and they left it there, stuck between the rocks, and then quitted the harbour.

So they were in sore straits for want of their anchor, and for the loss of the smith who could have made one for them. Then said Brendan to a priest of his company: "Do thou," said he, "the work of the smith for us to the end of a month." So Brendan blessed the hands of the priest, for he had never previously learnt smith's craft. Then, however, the priest made an admirable anchor, and there was never found either before or since anything to compare with it for excellence of workmanship.

The brother who was snatched away

Another day as Brendan was voyaging on the ocean he saw a great hellish mountain which appeared full of clouds and smoke about its summit. And the wind carried them with irresistible force to the shore of the island whereon the mountain was, so that the boat was close to land. And the brink of the island was of an appalling height, so that they could scarcely see the top of it, and it appeared full of firebrands and red sparks, and was as steep as a wall.

And one of the three brethren who had followed Brendan from the monastery, left the boat, and went to the edge of the brink; and he had not been long there when he shrieked a loud and piteous shriek, and said: "Alas, my father, for I am being carried away from you, and I have no power of returning to you."

And when the brethren saw this, great terror seized them, and they put out from land, and uttered a cry unto the heavenly Lord, saying: "*Miserere mei, Domine,*" that is, O Lord, have mercy upon us, have mercy upon us.

Brendan however looked upon him, and saw a multitude of demons round him, and he burning in their midst. And he said: "Alas, poor hapless one, for the end which thou hast brought on thyself, and on thy life."

And after this the wind swept them away, and they drove towards the south. And they looked back on the island, and saw it all on fire, belching out its flame into the air, and swallowing it again, so that the mountain seemed all one ball of fire.

The island of Paul the Hermit

One day when Brendan and his company were traversing the abyss, they saw an island in the distance. And when the brethren perceived it they steered their boat joyfully towards it. And Brendan said to them: "Do not exert yourselves immoderately, for it is seven years since we left our own land to this present Easter; and ye shall now shortly see a hermit in this island named Paul, who has not touched corporeal food or drink for three score years, and for a score of years he received sustenance from a certain animal."

When they came near the shore, they could not enter the island because of its steepness, for its banks were high and impracticable, and the island itself small and round all about, and there was no soil on the summit, but bare stony rock; and its height and breadth were equal. And after skirting the island they found an entry in the bank so narrow that there was scarcely room in it for the prow of the boat; and it was still more difficult to ascend into the island. And Brendan said to the brethren: "Wait here, till I come to you, for ye may not enter this island without the permission of God's special servant who is in it."

And when Brendan came to the summit of the island, he saw two caves fronting one another, and he saw small fountains dropping from the rock on the face of the caves. And when Brendan came in front of the caves, he saw an aged man coming to him out of one of them, who said: *"Ecce quam bonum,"* that is, It is clear that it is good for brethren to come together. And having said this he bade Brendan call the brethren from the boat.

When Brendan had done so, the servant of God kissed them all, and greeted them by their own names. And the brethren wondered greatly at the garb of the man, for he had no clothing except the hair of his head and his beard, and the hair of the rest of his body. And this hair was such that no snow was whiter than it owing to the great age of the holy man. But Brendan said, weeping and sobbing: "Alas for me, sinner that I am, to wear a monk's habit, and many monks with me in the same habit, while a man of angelic condition, though still in the body, sits naked, and untormented with vices of the flesh."

Paul, the servant of God, said to Brendan: "O honoured father, innumerable are the miracles which have been revealed to thee, which never

were revealed to any holy father before thee.
And thou sayest in thine heart, that thou art not
worthy to wear the habit of a monk! I say unto
thee, father, that thou art more than any monk
who is nourished and maintained by the labour
of his own hands. God hath fed and clothed thee
and the monks for seven years out of His own
secret treasure."

Brendan asked Paul how he came to that
island and place, and where he dwelt previously,
and how long he had endured that life. Paul
answered him, and said: "My father, I was
nourished in the monastery of Patrick for the
space of fifty years, having charge of the
cemetery of the brethren. And one day I asked
my dean to point out to me the burial place of
one whom I had to bury. And when he had
pointed it out to me, an unknown aged man
came to me, and said to me: 'Do not dig in that
place, brother, for that is the grave of another
man.' I said to him: 'Who art thou, Father?' He
answered: 'How is it thou dost not recognize
me, when I am thy abbot?' I said to him: 'Nay,
but Patrick is my abbot.' 'I am he,' said he, 'and
yesterday I departed from this world. And this is
my place of burial.'

"And after saying this, he then pointed out to

me another place, and said: 'Bury thy brother
there, and tell no one else what I have said to
thee. And tomorrow go to the sea, and there
thou shalt find a boat which will bear thee to the
place where thou wilt remain till the day of thy
death.' When morning came on the morrow, I
set out for the sea according to the father's
command, and found there as was promised me.
And entering into the boat I made a voyage of
three days and three nights, and then I ceased
rowing, and let the boat go as the wind might
carry it to land. And on the seventh day
afterwards I found this rock, and the boat came
to land on it. And after I had left the boat it
returned swiftly to its own land, and I remained
here from that day to this.

"And the first day that I came here there came
to me an animal, called otter, and brought me a
fish, and a flint to make a fire withal, carrying
them between its front feet while it walked on
its hind feet; and when it had laid these down
before me, it returned to its own place. And
when it had returned, I struck fire and kindled it
with the flint which had been left with me, and I
dressed the fish, and ate of it as much as sufficed
me. And the same messenger would come to me
every third day with this refreshment. And I

remained thus to the end of thirty years without lack of food or drink. And a stream of water would drop from the rock for me every Sunday, in which I would wash my hands, and drink a draught to quench my thirst.

"And afterwards I found these two caves, and the fountains, and these sustain me without substance of other food for the space of three score years, and I have been ninety years in the island, thirty years supported by fish, and sixty years supported by the fountain, and I was fifty years in my own land. And this is the sum of my years, one hundred and forty to this day; and I am still awaiting in this human body the day of my account."

After this the holy elder said: "Get ready, Brendan, to depart, and take some of the water of the fountain with you in your vessels; for the road before you is long, a journey of forty days to Easter Eve. And ye shall keep this Easter as ye have done in the other seven years, and afterwards ye shall reach the land which is more exceeding holy than any land, and ye shall remain there to the end of yet another forty days. And after that, God will bring you safe to your native land."

After this conversation Brendan bade farewell

to the man of God, and they received his
blessing, and departed in peace; and steered their
ship towards the south, and thus they were
during Lent. And the boat was carried hither
and thither on the face of the ocean, and they
had no food with them except the water which
they had brought from the island of the man of
God. And they were cheerful and free from
thirst and hunger for the space of three days
(that is, partaking of the water only once in three
days), till they reached the island of the procurator on the following Easter Eve.

And when the procurator saw them, he came
to the port to meet them with joy and great
gladness; and he took the hand of each of them
as they disembarked. And when they had
finished the office of Saturday, the procurator
brought them their supper; and when night
came upon them they embarked again, and the
procurator with them. And they found the great
beast in its accustomed place, and they sang the
praises of God that night, and said their Masses
in the morning.

And when they had finished their Masses, the
huge animal proceeded on its own business, and
they all standing on its back. When the brethren
perceived this, they all cried aloud, and said:

"Exaudi nos," that is, Listen to us, O God, our mighty Saviour.

But Brendan was exhorting them not to fear; and the whale went straight forward, till it reached the strand of the island called *the Isle of Birds;* and deposited them all there without loss of any of them. And they remained in that spot till the octave of Pentecost.

And when the feast of Pentecost was past, the procurator said to Brendan: "Embark in your boat now, and fill your bottles from the fount, and I will be with you and guide you, for ye cannot find the land ye are seeking, unless I am with you."

The island of the demon smithy

Another day as Brendan was traversing the ocean, he saw an island near him, hideous, dark, mountainous, and rocky, with a rugged summit, without trees or herbs, but full of houses like forges. When the holy father Brendan saw this, he said to the brethren at that time: "Dear brothers," said he, "I am much afraid of this island for you, and it is not my will to go there if we could avoid it; but the wind is driving us straight to it."

And they were not more than a small stone's

throw from it, when they heard the thunderous working of the bellows being blown, and the clang of the hammers as they smote the anvils. Great fear seized them, and the holy father raised his hand, and made the sign of the holy cross towards the four quarters of the heaven round about, and said: "Lord Jesus Christ, deliver us from the folk of this island." After this they saw a couple, hideously black like the colour of a smith's coal, coming out of the forges, as if they were going to do some work or other.

And when they saw God's people, they turned back again into the forges, and brought out two charges of molten iron, red hot, which they held with tongs in their hands, and rushing eagerly to the shore, they cast them at the boat. And this did no harm to them, for such was not God's will, for they passed over their heads some distance beyond the boat. After this God sent a following wind to Brendan's company from the side of the island. And out of the same forges there issued an innumerable, hideous and diabolic band, carrying fiery charges in tongs to cast at them. And where these charges struck the sea it boiled up high above them, like a cauldron or pot over a huge fire.

And as they could not do them any harm,

they returned to the forges, and set them all in a
red blaze, and began hurling the red-hot charges
at one another. And the cries and shrieks which
they uttered were heard after they were out of
sight. Thus God delivered His people from the
devil's folk, for it is clear that these all belonged
to the company of hell. And Brendan bade his
company to be of good cheer, and steadfast
faith, and to give thanks to God and to His
angels. And they did as the holy father, Brendan, bade them.

Contest of the two sea monsters
One day as Brendan and his company were
traversing the ocean, they saw a huge and
terrible fish coming towards them, throwing up
the waves on either side of him in his hurry to
get to the boat to swallow them up. When the
brethren saw this, they cried aloud to the
heavenly Lord, and said: "O Lord, who madest
man and the elements, deliver us."

And they began crying to Brendan in like
wise. Brendan said: "O Lord, who madest man
and the elements, deliver us, and deliver Thine
own people from yonder terrible monster."

And he said further: "Brothers, be not afraid;
and small is your confidence, for He who

delivered us from every danger, and He who has protected us continually, He will deliver us from the maw of yonder monster."

And the monster came in front of the boat, and reared itself on high above their heads. When Brendan saw this, he went into the prow of the boat, and lifted up his hands to heaven, and said these words: *"Domine, libera nos,"* that is, O Lord, save Thy people, as Thou saved David from the hands of Goliath, and Jonah from the belly of the whale.

And when he had finished this prayer, they saw another like monster coming from the west quarter to meet the first monster. And when it came up to it, it emitted a fiery ball from its gullet. And it waged war against the first monster.

When Brendan saw this, he said to the brethren: "Do you see, dear monks, the marvels of the Lord, and the obedience which the creature renders to the Creator?" And when he had said this to them, they saw the monster which had pursued Brendan rising in three pieces to the surface of the sea; and the monster that had done these deeds returned to the place whence it had come with triumphant victory.

The griffin with the great claws

One day as Brendan and the brethren were traversing a bay, they saw a terrible bird above their heads, a griffin with great claws, and it was fully as big as a mule or an ox. And when the brethren saw it they were seized with great fear and horror, and they said: "O father, help us speedily, for it is to devour us that yon terrible monster has come."

Brendan said: "Fear not, for He who has delivered you from every doubtful pass hitherto, will deliver us from this danger."

And as the griffin was stretching out its claw towards the brethren, the bird which had brought the branch to them came towards them, and fought with it, and overcame it. And when it had overcome it, it tore its eyes out of it, and its body fell into the sea before the brethren. And when they saw this they praised God greatly. And the aforesaid bird returned to the Isle of Ailbe afterwards.

The isle of the twelve Irishmen and the sea-cat

After this they rowed for a while over the ocean in a westerly direction, and found a pleasant little island with a number of fishermen in it. As they were going round it they saw in it a little stone church, in which was an aged man, pale and sorrowful, engaged in prayer. And he had neither flesh nor blood, but merely a thin miserable skin over his hard and yellow bones. Then that elder said: "Flee, Brendan, with all speed," said he. "For there is here now a sea-cat as big as a young ox or a three-year-old horse, which has thriven on the fish of the sea and of this island; beware of it now."

They betake them to their boat, and row over the ocean with all their might. As they were thus, they saw the monstrous sea-cat swimming after them; each of its two eyes was as big as a cauldron, it had tusks like a boar, sharp-pointed bristles, the maw of a leopard, the strength of a lion, and the rage of a mad dog. Then each of them began to pray to God by reason of the great fear which seized them. Then said Brendan: "O God Almighty," said he, "keep off Thy monsters from us, that they may not reach us."

Then a great sea whale rose up between them and the cat-monster, and each of them set to work to try and drown the other in the depths of the sea, and neither of them ever appeared again. Then Brendan and his company gave thanks to God, and turned back again to the place where the elder was. And the elder wept for the greatness of the joy which possessed him, and said: "I am of the men of Erin," said he, "and twelve of us were there when we came on our pilgrimage, and we brought that bestial sea-cat with us, and we were very fond of it; and it grew afterwards enormously, but it never hurt any of us. And now of our original company eleven have died, and I am left alone, waiting for thee to give me the body and blood of Christ, that therewith I may go to heaven."

He revealed to them afterwards the little country which they were seeking, that is *the Land of Promise*. And after receiving the body and blood of Christ, the elder went to heaven. He was buried there beside his brethren with great reverence, and with psalms and hymns, in the name of the Father, and of the Son, and of the Holy Ghost.

The finding of the land of promise
One day when Brendan and his company were traversing and searching the sea, they happened upon the little country which they had been seeking for seven years, to wit, *the Land of Promise;* as it says in the proverb: *He that seeketh, findeth.* When they came near to this land, and

they were minded to take harbour there, they heard the voice of a certain elder speaking to them and saying: "O much travailed men, O holy pilgrims, O ye who look for the heavenly rewards, O ever-toilsome life in labouring and waiting for this country, stay a little from your labour now."

When they had remained a little while at rest, the elder said to them: "Dear brothers in Christ," said he, "do ye not perceive this glorious and lovely land, on which never was spilt the blood of man, and in which it is not fitting that any sinner or evil-doer should be buried? Leave now everything that ye have in your boat, except the few clothes that ye have on, and come up hither."

When they came to land, each of them kissed the other, and the elder wept greatly for his exceeding joy. "Search and see," said he, "the borders and regions of Paradise, where will be found health without sickness, pleasure without contention, union without quarrel, dominion without interruption, attendance of angels, feasting without diminution, meadows sweet in scent as fair blessed flowers. Happy indeed is he whom Brendan son of Findlug shall summon thither to join him," said the same elder, "to

inhabit for ever and ever the island in which we
are."

But when they saw Paradise amid the waves
of the sea, they marvelled and were astonished at
the wonders of God, and His power when they
saw these wonders. Now the elder was on this
wise, without any human clothing at all, but his
body was covered with a white down like a
dove or sea-mew, and his speech was almost like
that of an angel. They celebrated Terce after
ringing the bell, with giving of thanks to God,
and with their minds fixed on God. But they did
not dare to ask any question.

Then said the elder: "Let each of you pray
privately without speech of any to other of you,
for this land is holy and angelic, and moreover
sin commonly attaches to speech, for often in
old-world fables is there either sorrow or idle
joy." "We agree in sooth," said the folk. When
they had remained thus for a while, the elder
came to them and said: "Let us celebrate the
midday office (Sext)," said he; and when they
had finished celebrating the midday office,
Brendan asked that elder: "Is it God's will for
me," said he, "that I should remain here till the
day of doom?"

But the elder answered him on this wise: *"He*

who shall seek his own will opposes the will of God.
And it is sixty years," said he, "since I came
hither, and the food of angels has fed me all that
time. And my body was wellnigh wasted away
with old age. But it was not here that I grew
old, but I continue at the age at which I was
when I came here. And Christ bade me remain
here to wait for thee another thirty years in
addition to that first thirty. And now it is time
for me to go to heaven, for thou hast come to
me. And when ye have celebrated None, depart
to your own land, and instruct the men of Erin,
for crimes and sins shall be corrected by thee.
And Christ said to me at this hour of None that
thou shouldst come to this land with thy family,
thy monks and nuns, together with the saints of
Erin, seven years before the judgement, and
with that marvellous anchor which the priest
made for thee."

When they had celebrated None, the bird
which was wont to minister their refreshment to
them previously, came bringing a half loaf of
wheaten bread and a morsel of fish for each of
them. When they had taken their refreshment,
they gave thanks to God. And when the elder
had taken the body of Christ, His flesh and
blood, he sent his spirit to heaven, and they

buried his body then with great honour and marvellous respect.

After this mutual converse Brendan and his monks proceeded to their boat. And they departed over the great-waved sea, and nothing unusual is narrated of their journeyings till they came to eastern Aran (Aranmore), having been two years on this voyage, and five on the former voyage, so that they were seven years altogether on the two voyages seeking the Land of Promise; as a certain learned man said:

Seven years in all were they
On the voyage — fair was the band —
Seeking the land of promise
With its flocks, a strong subtle turn.

And they found it at last
In the high meads of the ocean,
An island rich, everlasting, undivided,
Abounding in salmon, fair and beauteous.

When they reached Aran, they received a great welcome there, such as Christ and His Apostles might receive. And they related their story and adventures to the people of Aran, from first to last. When Enda and Pupa and their companions heard the story, they wept greatly from the excess of the joy which possessed them. And the people tried to detain Brendan, and agreed to give him a recompense if he would only stay with them. Brendan said to them: "Not here shall be my resurrection," said he; and he declined to remain there. They were the space of a month there after their labour in rowing.

At the end of this time and season Brendan and his company left in Aran the boat and its anchor, and themselves proceeded to Ireland, and took harbour at Inis da Droma in the sea of Limerick. They remained there, and were four days and four nights without refreshment of food or drink. And four of the holy band died there through the length of the fast which befell them, and they were buried there with honour and great reverence.

It is remarkable that the finding of the Promised Land of the Saints appears to have brought no consequences for the further life of Brendan. Indeed his deeds now seem to be altogether on a lower plane. Stories are told of acts almost of vengeance and of actions amounting to trickery.

One story tells how Brendan turned a man, Dobarchu by name, into an otter because he had killed some of Brendan's oxen which had strayed into Dobarchu's meadow. Another story tells how the saints of Ireland came to quarrel with King Diarmait and how they took part in a fasting match with the king. Brendan intervened on behalf of the saints, by magic causing some of Diarmait's men to be drowned, and by working a trick upset the king's fast thus enabling the saints to get the upper hand.

In a fit of anger Brendan sent a man to his death in a storm. Because of this act, Brendan's foster-mother, Ita, advised him to cross the sea to a foreign land. The crossing took three years and Brendan landed in Britain where he built a monastery. On his return to Ireland, he was to build another monastery, this time at Clonfert, which he said was to be his resting-place. Later he travelled to Gaul. In both these countries he performed good works and miracles. In between journeys, he returned to Ireland and on one occasion he had a notable conversation with St Brigid. Among other incidents relating to this time of Brendan's life, we find the following delightful story written in a specially lively style:

One time Brendan son of Findlug was at Clonfert on Easter Day in the seventh year before his death. The canonical hours had been celebrated in the church, the sermon preached, and Mass said. When midday came, the monks went to the refectory; and Brendan was left alone in the church.

The brethren then began the order of the refectory. There was a young clerk with them, and he had a little harp in his hand. He began to play to them, and they blessed him for it.

"I should be wondrous pleased now," said the young clerk, "if Brendan would admit me into the church, that I might play three strains to him."

"He will not admit thee," said the monks. "For seven years past Brendan has never smiled, and has never listened to any music in the world; but two balls of wax tied together with a thread are always on the book in front of him. And whenever he hears any music, he puts the balls into his ears."

"I will go," said the young clerk, "to play the harp to him."

So the young clerk went away, with his harp ready tuned in his hand.

"Open," said the young clerk.

"Who is there?" said Brendan.

"A young clerk to play the harp to thee," said he.

"Play outside," said Brendan.

"If thou dost not mind, I should be glad if thou wouldst admit me into the church to thee."

"Very well," said he, "open the door."

The young clerk set his harp on the floor between his feet. Brendan puts the two balls of wax into his two ears.

"I don't like," said the young clerk, "to play to thee on that wise, unless thou take the wax out."

"I will do so," said he; and he put the balls of wax on the book before him. Then the clerk played three strains to him.

"A blessing on thee, young clerk," said Brendan, "and the music of heaven to thee hereafter."

Then he put the balls into his ears, for he did not care to listen to any music of this world.

"Why dost thou not listen to music?" said the young clerk. "Is it because thou deemest it bad?"

"Nay, young clerk," said he, "not that. But seven years ago this very day I was in this church after Mass and sermon here; all the young clerks had gone to the refectory, and I was left here alone. A great yearning for my Lord seized me after my communion. While in that state, fear and trembling took me, and I saw a bird on the window, which settled on the altar.

I could not look upon it for the sun-bright beams that were around it.

" 'Give us thy blessing, O cleric,' said he.

" 'May God bless thee,' said I. 'And who is it?' said I.

" 'Michael the angel,' said he, 'come to converse with thee.'

" 'I thank God indeed,' said I, 'and why art thou come?'

" 'To sain thee, and to play to thee, for thy Lord.'

" 'Thou art welcome to me,' said I.

"He drew his beak across the wattle of his wing. And I listened till the same hour on the following day, and then he bade me farewell."

Here Brendan drew his bookmark across the neck of the harp.

"Does that seem sweet to thee, young clerk? I declare before God," said Brendan, "not sweeter to me is any music in the world, compared with that music, than the noise made by this bookmark. And take my blessing, and heaven be thine in return for playing to me."

The death of Brendan

rendan went to visit his sister Brig at the fort of Aed son of Eochaid, which is now called Enach Duin. So then, after traversing sea and land, after raising dead men, healing lepers, blind, deaf, lame, and all kinds of sick folk, after founding many cells, and monasteries, and holy churches, after appointing abbots and masters, after blessing cataracts and estuaries, after consecrating districts and tribes, after putting down crimes and sins, after great perils by sea and land, after expelling demons and vices, after pre-eminence in pilgrimage and ascetic devotion, after performance of mighty works and miracles too numerous to mention, St Brendan drew near to the day of his death.

Then said Brendan to the brethren after Mass on the Sunday, and after receiving the body of Christ and His blood: "God," said he, "is calling me to the eternal kingdom; and my body must be taken to Clonfert, for there will be attendance of angels there, and there will be my resurrection. Make a small chariot, and let a single one of you go with it to convey my body, lest, if it were a large waggon with a numerous attendance, the tribes should notice it, and dispute for my body. And a young man with only one eye, the left, to speak precisely, will meet the bearer of my body, namely Cuirrine son of Setna. And he will say to the brother who has the corpse: 'Is that the body of the Saint that thou hast?' he will say in a gruff voice: 'among us shall his resurrection be; give up the body.'

"Then," said Brendan, "let the brother offer Cuirrine a mass of gold which he will take from the ground, to let him go. The man will say that he will not let him go for that. 'Thou shalt have the kingship,' shall the brother say to him, 'thyself and thy seed after thee. Let me go. And this is a sign to thee; I was talking to Brendan today how thou wouldst get the kingship.' 'No,' he will say. Then, shall the brother say: 'Thou shalt have heaven and earth.' And he will let him go," said Brendan, "after this for the sake of these three things, the gold, the kingship, and heaven. Then the brother will bless him, and he will depart altogether."

When he had finished saying all this, he blessed the brethren and his sister Brig, and when he reached the threshold of the church, he

said: *"In manus tuas, Domine."* Then he sent forth
his spirit, having completed ninety-three years;
as the prophet said:

The age of Brendan who was without crime,
Who was sage, and prophet, and poet;
Ninety-three years exactly
He lived amid great peril.

It was five hundred and eighty-one years from
the Incarnation of Christ, the Son of God, to the
death of Brendan; as was said:

From the birth of Mary's Son,
To Brendan's dying hour,
Was a glorious eighty-one,
And then five hundred more.

And his feast is kept on the sixteenth day of the
month of January (read: May) to speak precisely.

The body of Brendan was placed on the
chariot on the morrow, as Brendan had said,
and a single brother went with it. Cuirrine mac
Setna met him, and said to him as St Brendan
had foretold. The body of Brendan was then
brought to Clonfert and buried there with great
honour and reverence, with psalms and hymns

and spiritual songs, in honour of the Father, and of the Son, and of the Holy Ghost.

I entreat the mercy of Almighty God through the intercession of St Brendan, that we may all reach the Unity of the Holy Trinity; may we win it, may we dwell in it for ever and ever. Amen.

Colophon

In the convent of the brethren on the Drowse I rewrote this life of Brendan from the paper copy which I previously made from the book which Siograid Ua Maelconaire (Seery O'Mulconry) wrote for Rose daughter of Aed Duv, son of Aed Roe O'Donnell, wife of Niall the younger, son of Art, son of Conn O'Neill in the place of Sen-Caislen beside Sliab Truim. The age of Christ, as the writer shows, was then 1536. And the age of Christ now is March 27, 1629. I am the poor friar, Michael O'Clery.